THE EMPIRE STATE BUILDING BOOK

THE EMPIRE STATE BUILDING BOOK

Written by Jonathan Goldman
Designed by Michael Valenti

A Stepping Stone Book produced
by Steven Heller, Sarah Jane Freymann,
and Steven Schwartz

St. Martin's Press
New York

Acknowledgments

Thanks, first of all, to the producers of this book—Steve Heller, Sarah Jane Freymann and Steve Schwartz—for inviting me to write it. Thanks especially to Steve Schwartz, who, throughout the project, miraculously managed to be both a very good editor and a very good friend. Thanks to Mike Valenti for designing the book and for loving the Empire State Building so dearly. Thanks to Bill Suchanek and Tim Sullivan at the Empire State itself, to Colleen MacDonald at Rubenstein Associates, and to Bill Morace at the Carpenters District Council for help with the research. And to Kimble Mead, Suzanne Slesin, Charles Churchward, John Beader and Edward Spiro, who have contributed photos and other ephemera to use in the book.

Finally, thanks to my cat, Muffin, who kept me company, to my daughter, Laurie, who did without my company, and to my wife, Adrienne, who was endlessly understanding.

To Adrienne and Laurie

Library of Congress Cataloging in Publication Data
Goldman, Jonathan
The Empire State Building Book.
1. New York (City). Empire State Building.
I. Freymann, Sarah Jane, joint author
II. Heller, Steven, joint author
III. Schwartz, Steven, joint author
IV. Valenti, Michael, joint author
V. Title.
F128.8.E46H44 974.7'1 80-14185
ISBN 0-312-24455-X
ISBN 0-312-24456-8 (pbk.)

CONTENTS

CORREOS D͏͏ᴸ ECUADOR

AEREO

CONCURRENCIA A LA EXPOSICION
INTERNACIONAL DE NEW YORK 1939

10 — DIEZ — 10
CENTAVOS

THOMAS DE LA RUE & COY., LTD. LONDRES.

THE UMPIRE STATE BUILDING

If, like the author, you grew up in Brooklyn and loved baseball, you might have started out thinking it was called the Umpire State Building—not such a bad name for a building with that kind of authority. If you went to watch older kids fly model planes in the lots on Flatlands Avenue, you saw the thing clear across Brooklyn, fifteen miles away and still huge and imposing. When you went to Manhattan you discovered the unique and delicious vertigo you could produce by standing right next to the Empire State and staring straight up. You and your friend said, "It's *so tall!*" and pummeled each other's backs because you knew you didn't really have the words to say it. When you got to the top, you shouted, unembarrassed, and with a sense of discovery at least the equal of Christopher Columbus': "Look at the cars down there! They look like ants!"

It turns out you didn't have to grow up anywhere near New York to share the sentiments—the building belongs to the world. Little replicas of it have turned up in the bazaars of remote villages in India (next to little Charlie Chaplin dolls). On islands off Alaska, Aleut Indian children have pumped visitors for the real facts about King Kong and the Empire State Building. Whatever his feelings about empires and empire states, Fidel Castro grinned from ear to ear when he visited the building.

If to a child the Empire State has some of the qualities of an oversized toy, to an adult it is inevitably a symbol—an icon, at the very least, of New York City. While the Statue of Liberty stands for the dream of New York as the safe haven at the end of every immigrant's wanderings, the Empire State says something about the power and style of the town. It has something to do with the Machine, much to do with business, and still more to do with elegance and pride. Down in the lobby, the illuminated glass panels showing the Eight Wonders of the World may seem like the work of a cut-rate Cecil B. De Mille, and the little elevator you take up to eighty-six may inspire more nostalgia than awe, but all that changes at the top. At the top of the Empire State it is hard to believe that anyone would dare whisper the world *default* in relation to New York City. It is even hard to believe that those gray ribbons of streets down there have so much as the tinest pothole. The sight speaks only of grandeur and might. And the two towers you have to look *up* at don't really diminish the Empire State at all. The World Trade Center is just a couple of tall buildings; the Empire State Building is a monument.

Icon or toy, the building stands on a very choice two acres of Manhattan turf—and the land has its own story. It has figured prominently in the city's history, housing a population that zoomed from zero to 35,000 in the century and a half it took for wilderness to become Gotham.

Chapter 1

GEORGE WASHINGTON SCHLEPPED HERE

Where the Empire State Building now stands at 34th Street and Fifth Avenue, the American Revolution very nearly fizzled out. In September 1776, following a disastrous defeat in the Battle of Long Island, George Washington tried to position his troops to defend Manhattan. The idea wasn't really his own. Many had advised him to burn New York (then a city of 20,000) because it was indefensible, but Congress wanted the city held. Washington had some 19,000 men, most of them green Continentals just drafted in Connecticut, while General Howe had 31,000 well-trained British regulars, at least 10,000 seamen, and an additional force of Hessians. One hundred thirty British warships made Lower New York Bay look like "a forest of pine trees with their branches trimmed."

Washington's troops, scattered over sixteen miles of terrain, were weakest in the middle, which is where the British attacked. On September 15, 1776, under cover of a tremendous bombardment from their ships, the British began their landing at Kip's Bay, where present-day 34th Street meets the East River. The Connecticut militiamen defending the shore instantly ran away without firing a shot. ("The dastardly behaviour of the Rebels . . . sinks below remark," wrote the Secretary to the British admiral.) And so the rout began.

When Washington himself arrived on the scene, he found panic-stricken soldiers fleeing north toward him, in the direction of Harlem Heights. He took up a position on a knoll where the New York Public Library now stands at Fifth Avenue and 42nd Street and tried to turn the tide. Once the British came into view, though, all discipline evaporated, and the entire American army dissolved into a terrified mob charging north. Colonel Tench Tilghman wrote that Washington "laid his Cane over many of the Officers who shewed their men the Example of running." Others reported a sort of tantrum in

The bombardment of Kip's Bay

which he called his troops "scum" and "cowards." The more traditional picture has him throwing his hat to the ground and exclaiming, "Good God, have I got such troops as these?" and "Are these the men with which I am to defend America?" His frenzy of rage had no effect on the troops, and it later left Washington himself in a strange, exhausted stupor. Although a detachment of British was approaching, the Commander-in-Chief moped in his saddle, almost alone amid piles of cast-off muskets, powder horns, hats and coats. His head was bowed and his eyes unfocused. Finally, an aide had to grab Washington's bridle and lead him out of danger.

After this fiasco, later known as the Battle of Kip's Bay or the Battle

"Old Put" (General Israel Putnam) beating a retreat

of the Cornfield, the British could have marched straight across Manhattan on the level of 34th Street (passing the site of the Empire State Building) and very neatly trapped the 3,500 American troops under General Israel Putnam still remaining in the southern tip of the island. Much ink has flowed over General Howe's failure to do just this. The American legend blames the British delay on the wiles of a certain Mary Murray. Mrs. Murray and her husband Robert owned a large farm on Inclenberg Heights (later Murray Hill), and on the afternoon of September 15th she invited General Howe and his officers to her lavish home to sample her cakes and her old Madeira. Knowing that ten minutes' difference might mean the end to General Putnam and his troops, Mary Murray charmed the British general staff into dawdling a full two hours, joking with them about the sad fate of her "American friends." Meanwhile, Putnam and his men slipped through and joined Washington at Harlem Heights. Mary Murray, patriot and siren, even inspired a play. Robert Sherwood's *Small War on Murray Hill* (1955) had her tempting General Howe with more than cakes and wine. She offered a warm bath, steamed clams, pheasant, lemon souffle and finally herself. (She was in fact a Quaker matron with twelve children.) New York Mayor Fiorello LaGuardia also honored her in 1938 when he christened a Staten Island ferryboat the *Mary Murray*.

Although Washington and his troops were able to regroup and then to repulse the British at Harlem Heights, New York City had been lost and it remained British headquarters for another seven years. But the value of the prize plummeted on September 20, 1776, when a fire ravaged large parts of the city. When he heard about it, a recovered General Washington commented, "Providence, or some good honest fellow, has done more for us than we were disposed to do for ourselves."

At the time Washington's troops were scurrying across it, most of the site of the Empire State Building was virgin common-land belonging to the city. The western slice of the site, though, had already been granted in a 1686 patent to "Francisco Bastian, a Negro." His fifteen acre, fourteen rod property was bounded on "the West by the Highway or Road (now Broadway) . . . and (on) the East by a Swamp." In 1716 his family sold the land to Garrit Oncklebagg, a silversmith.

The rest of the Empire State Building site was not granted until 1799, when John Thomson bought an untilled twenty-acre tract for $2,400 and began to farm it. In those days the land was still quiet country, well north of the city.

Although stretched across the present city plan on a slight bias, the Thomson farm virtually comprised the six blocks now bounded by Broadway and Sixth Avenue on the west, Madison Avenue on the east and Thirty-third and Thirty-sixth streets on the south and north.

The land was intersected by Sunfish Creek, which rose in a spring in Fifty-seventh street, just west of Broadway, and emptied into the "Sun Fish Pond" at the foot of the present Park Avenue. It was one of the many watercourses of Manhattan Island now completely lost. The stream approached the Empire State property from a point in Thirty-fourth street . . . It was joined in the middle of the skyscraper site by another shorter brook which was fed by

Venus and Mars: Mary Murray and General Howe

a spring . . . This junction of the two brooks formed a natural fishing hole, and judging from letters and diaries still extant many a fine mess of sunfish and eels were hooked where visitors are now entering the tower express elevators.

New York Sun, May 1, 1931

In 1825 Thomson put his farm on the market with the following notice:

A new and convenient house, barn, and several out-buildings, together with 20 acres of land, situated in the heart of New York Island, along the Middle Road, near the 3-mile stone, about ½ mile north from Chelsea Village. The land is fertile, partly-wooded, and well-watered, and eminently suitable for the raising of various produce, profitably disposed of to the opulent families of the City. It is confidently expected by those whose opinions are conceded to be found, that the rapid growth of the City and the villages of Greenwich and Chelsea will soon cause the value of the Aforesaid Land to be greatly enhanced.

–Jno. Thomson

The land was bought by Thomas and Margaret Lawrance, who then sold it to Charles Lawton for $10,000. In two years' time, Lawton doubled his money when he sold the twenty acres to William B. Astor for $20,500. One hundred years later, that same land would sell for a cool $8,000,000 an acre.

13

Chapter 2

MAUVE ORCHIDS

It would take one century for the world's tallest building to sprout from the site of Farmer Thomson's cornfield. In those hundred years, New York, which at first had huddled down at the southern tip of Manhattan, pressed steadily northward until it filled and overflowed the whole island. During that century, the Empire State Building land belonged to the most formidable of the early New York clans, the Astors.

The Empire State Building site: the Waldorf Hotel overshadows Mrs. Astor's mansion

The Astor dynasty got its start when John Jacob Astor, a penniless butcher's son from Waldorf, Germany, landed in America in 1784 and proceeded to dominate the fur trade clear across North America. He and his son William Backhouse Astor plowed most of their fur profits into New York City real estate, a timely move that made William B. the landlord—some say the slumlord—of New York City. By 1865 his holdings would be large enough to make his income tax bill $1,300,000. It was this same William Backhouse Astor who in 1827 had bought the Thomson farm for $20,500.

The whole Astor clan was still based down at Astor Place, near Greenwich Village, when an 1849 slum riot changed Astor Place to "Massacre Place" and drove the family uptown. In 1856, William B. Astor's two sons both chose the Thomson farm as the site for their mansions. When other rich families followed their lead, the neighboring stretch of Fifth Avenue swiftly became "Millionaire's Row," the home of the "Knickerbocracy."

Although old John Jacob Astor was not famous for his breeding—at one dinner he wiped his dirty hands on the white dress of his host's daughter—his grandchildren were already the possessors of (by the American time scale) *old* money, and their generation helped consoli-

Caroline Schermerhorn Astor

date upper class life into a formal round of balls, operas, dinners and summers at Newport. It was in fact his grandson's wife, Caroline Schermerhorn Astor, who personally invented "The 400," that exclusive inner circle of Gotham society, and she did it from her mansion on the old Thomson farm at 350 Fifth Avenue, the address of the Empire State Building.

No one describes Caroline Schermerhorn Astor as having particular beauty or wit, but she did have blue enough blood (on one side she could trace her ancestry back to James I of Scotland) and a fierce enough hunger for power. Her husband, William B. Astor II, found life more entertaining elsewhere, so in her social organizing she substituted as her lieutenant one Ward McAllister, a Southern dandy with plenty of blood and breeding but not much money. McAllister, who had been well received in London society, dreamed of an American aristocracy just as formal and exclusive as the European. He was further qualified by disliking Jews and Catholics just as much as Mrs. Astor did. Together they established the Patriarch's Ball, an annual bash sponsored by the twenty-five "leading" families—Astors, Schermerhorns, Langdons, Kanes, Livingstons, Van Rensselaers and others— all of them graced with old money as well as English or Dutch colonial pedigrees.

"The 400," as a name for the Knickerbocracy, is usually explained by the fact that Mrs. Astor's ballroom at 350 Fifth Avenue could hold just that number. It actually held more than that, and when McAllister was asked to name "The 400," he couldn't do it. Wherever it came from, the name stuck, especially with the millions of newspaper readers hungry for the smallest crumbs from their tables. Hollywood and its version of royalty didn't exist yet, so it was Mrs. Astor and her court who provided the copy. Women in Boise knew the very next day whether Mrs. Astor wore green velvet or purple satin the night before.

Who could join the club? There were hundreds of rich families in New York. When could you say that their raw new money had mellowed like fine Bordeaux into noble old money? It was Mrs. Astor's duty to open the gates to the few, while holding back the hordes of vulgar *nouveaux riches* pressing for acceptance. Of course, there were some theoretical problems in meshing hereditary aristocracy with democracy. One wit proposed a kind of solution:

In England the matter of precedence at dinners is simplicity itself. The Sovereign precedes an ambassador, who precedes the Archbishop of Canterbury, who precedes a duke, who precedes an earl, a marquis, a viscount, a bishop, a baron, etc.: but in America the matter is a much more perplexing one.

The author of this brochure respectfully suggests the following scheme of American dinner precedence: Let an opera box count 6 points; steam yacht 5; town house 5; country house 4; motors 3 each; every million dollars 2; tiara 1; good wine cellar 1; ballroom in town house 1; a known grandparent of either sex ½; culture ⅛. By this system, a woman of culture with four known grandparents and a million dollars will have a total of 4⅛. She will, of course, be forced to follow in the wake of a lady with a town house and a tiara (6); who, in turn, will trail after a woman with a steam yacht and two motors (11). The

Mrs. Astor's art gallery-ballroom

highest known total is about 100; the lowest, about ⅛. The housekeeper may arrange the totals, and the hostess can then send the guests in according to their listed quotations.
      –Francis Crowninshield, "Manners for the Metropolis: An Entrance Key to the Fantastic Life of the 400."

In whatever order they entered, none of Mrs. Astor's dinner guests went away hungry. They dined from gold plates on such delicacies as terrapin, or turtle, and the full menu might read:

Chaud
Consommé à la Princesse
Croquettes de volaille St. Cloud
Térapene
Filet de boeuf aux champignons
Canard Canvas-back Rôti
Salade de laitue et céleri
Froid
Galantine de perdreau aux truffes
Chaud-froid de caille a la Richelieu
Aspic de pâté de fois gras en bellevue
Pâté de gibier à la St. Hubert
Salade de volaille
Sandwiches assorti

In the 1890's "The 400" and their revels were gradually transplanted further uptown. Mrs. Astor's neighbor and nephew, William Waldorf Astor, did all he could to speed up this process. William owned the adjacent house on the old Thomson farm site. He couldn't stand his Aunt Caroline, and it was largely out of spite that he had his mansion at 33rd and Fifth torn down and replaced with a hotel— the Waldorf (named for his great-grandfather's village in Germany). Although it was the most elegant hotel in America, to *the* Mrs. Astor it could only be a "glorified tavern" and no fitting neighbor for her and her son (John Jacob Astor IV—later distinguished as the richest man on the Titanic). John Jacob Astor IV threatened to retaliate on cousin William by replacing their mansion with the largest stable in New York. He and his mother, of course, ordered a new palace further up Fifth Avenue, where most of the Knickerbocracy had already removed, but instead of a stable, he decided to top his cousin by building a hotel of his own—even larger than the Waldorf. His was called the Astoria. Negotiations produced a deal in which the Waldorf and the Astoria were fully interconnected, but all corridors could be instantly sealed off if family squabbles ever got in the way of good business.

And so was born the original Waldorf-Astoria Hotel. 350 Fifth Avenue retained its Astor cachet, but now, for a price, a wider public could sit down to its terrapin. The building itself, in German-Renaissance style, boasted sumptuous period rooms, a complete replica of an Astor dining room, a promenade called Peacock Alley, and a famous Men's Cafe. Newly-elected presidents and world-class generals celebrated their victories there. Li Hung Chang (Viceroy of China), the Crown Prince of Siam, Lord Kitchener of Khartoum, General Pershing, King Albert and Queen Elizabeth of Belgium, and Edward, Prince of Wales, all signed the register. But it was royalty American-style that really dominated the Waldorf—John Mack, the Asphalt King; Fritze Heinze, the Copper King; Hermann Frasch, the Sulphur King; not to mention J. Pierpont Morgan, Henry Clay Frick, George Jay Gould and Chauncey Depew.

By the 1890's, the area surrounding the Waldorf-Astoria, which included the theatres and the posh restaurants and bars on nearby Broadway and Sixth Avenue, had come to be known as the "Tenderloin."

The "tenderloin," a goal of every ambitious police captain, acquired its sobriquet when Inspector Alexander ("Clubber") Williams, took it over and declared that he had eaten chuck steak long enough and now would enjoy some tenderloin. It was the haunt of the old-time "actor, pugilist and turfman," and as the theatres pushed up Sixth Avenue, Thirty-fourth street with its junction of horse-car lines was becoming the focus of the show world.
–New York Sun, May 1, 1931

The tenderloin sported some of the biggest spenders of all time. It was there that C.K.G. Billings entertained his friends at Sherry's Restaurant, where, for novelty, they were served on horseback for $250 a plate. Another host imported four swans from Brooklyn's Prospect Park and had a thirty-foot pond constructed on the table. (Although the birds were drugged, they attacked the dinner, as well as the guests, ferociously.) At one of Diamond Jim Brady's Tenderloin soirees, the guests put away an average of one case of Mumm's champagne per person. Still, the next day Jim's friend Lillian Russell took her usual spin on the bike he had given her—it was gold-plated, with mother-of-pearl handlebars and spokes covered in diamonds, emeralds, rubies and sapphires (cost: $10,000).

The Waldorf-Astoria itself was the capital of the Tenderloin, and it was there that in 1897 the Bradley-Martins, a couple from upstate New York, threw the most expensive party in American history. Their own press release described how the Waldorf ballrooms would be decorated:

. . . five mirrors on the north side of the ballroom richly but not heavily garlanded in a curtain effect by mauve orchids and the feathery plemusa vine; garlands will be hung irregularly across the mirrors to loop onto the capitals of the columns

separating the mirrors; the chandeliers on each column will be decorated with orchids, and suspended from each chandelier will be a Rosalind-like pocket filled with Louis XVI roses and ferns. Roses will fall in showers over the balcony and will festoon the columns, not a space on the balcony, wall, or column that will not be festooned, banked, showered with bride, American beauty, and pink roses, or lilies-of-the-valley or orchids. The profusion of mauve orchids will stream carelessly to the floor, like the untied bonnet strings of a thoughtless child.

Meanwhile, upstairs in his suite, John "Bet-a Million" Gates was sitting down to poker with a few pals. In Gates' game, a gent might get up $150,000 lighter than he sat down.

Business was transacted at the Waldorf kitchens on the same scale as the festivities. Morning prices on the New York Stock Exchange rose and fell with the prior evening's talk at the Men's Cafe. It was at the Men's Cafe, too, and in John Gates' suite, that plans were laid for the U.S. Steel Corporation, the first billion-dollar business in the country. It was in Room 1162 that the Panama Canal project was laid out. It was back in the Men's Cafe that one James A. Patten tried to corner the market on wheat and Daniel J. Sully the market on cotton. No wonder, then, that a famed concoction of the Waldorf kitchens was something called *sweetbreads financier*.

For all the concentrated wealth under its roof, the Waldorf-Astoria itself finally became the victim of financial pressures. By the late 1920's, the land it stood on was simply too valuable for such a low-rise building (seventeen stories). Prime property like that called for a skyscraper. The hotel would be reincarnated further uptown on Park Avenue.

The bid that won the Waldorf-Astoria property came from John Jacob Raskob and his partners in the construction of the Empire State Building. When the news reached the papers, there were sentimental outpourings from all sides about the not-so-old hotel, and much bidding for the furnishings, especially the beds in which hundreds of couples had spent their wedding nights. Then one day a truck drove "through the wide door which had received presidents and princes . . . thrust its great bulk into the lobby . . . churned across the floor, then turned and roared down Peacock Alley, down that proud corridor lined with gold mirrors and velvet draperies." Before serious wrecking began, though, Raskob set about removing some choice marble pillars he wanted for his own summer home. But at the first stroke of the saw, the columns crumbled into a fine white powder. They were made of painted plaster.

Last days of the Waldorf ballroom   19

Chapter 3

GARGANTUA MEETS SIEGFRIED

O n the lofty min-arets of Manhattan there stands day and night an invisible muezzin who calls the faithful to the worship of Mammon and Speed. For our religion is a practical pantheism, with energy as the Eternal Substance.

We are the super-city. We are the Nibelungen of the West. We possess the Magic Rhine gold, which is the Holy Grail of Man's desire.

We are Gargantua and Siegfried. The old gods across the sea are graying. Already their Goetterdaemmerung has begun.

Come we, the newer Titans: and we are not yet pubescent.

In the fire and fury of our materialism we are dreaming of diviner Brunnhildes, Helenas and Aphrodites.

Out of matter comes mind; out of New York Athens shall rise again!

–Benjamin de Casseres, "New York: Matter Triumphalis," 1925

While the old Waldorf-Astoria was still flourishing at 350 Fifth Avenue, a new Manhattan was springing up around it. In the forty-odd years after 1890, to the sound of the jackhammer, the car horn, and the stock ticker, the city burst its seams. Bridges were flung across both rivers, the subway blasted up the length of Manhattan, the telephone linked to London, the radio to every home. The dirigible came to visit, the automobile and airplane to stay, and four-and-a-half million new inhabitants, many of them straight off the boat, jammed some streets until they were denser than Bombay's. Most of all, the city burst upward from its bedrock to heights no city had ever approached. In 1890, church steeples stood out on the skyline; as early as 1913, the cathedrals served folks of another persuasion:

When seen at nightfall bathed in electric light as with a garment or in the lucid air of a summer morning piercing space like a battlement of the paradise which St. John beheld, it inspires feelings too deep even for tears. I looked upon it and at once cried out, "The Cathedral of Commerce."

-Reverend S. Parker Cadman on the sixty-story Woolworth Building

The Home Insurance Building   *The Tower Building*

The Flatiron Building, The Times Building, The City Investing Co. Building

The Singer Building, The Woolworth Building, The Chrysler Building

Skyscraper Manhattan rose as the answer to a very simple question: How do you cram the business capital of a huge nation onto twenty-two square miles of granite isle? By 1880 technology had come up with its piece of the answer: build up. Tall towers—lighthouses, donjons, campaniles—had been around for hundreds of years, but none of them had much in the way of floor space. It wasn't until the 19th century that architects finally figured out how to float a board room in the clouds. The key was the iron or steel skeleton frame, an innovation that owed something to a water lily, to a birdcage, and to a bridge.

Water lily

Joseph Paxton took the first step in England, toward the middle of Queen Victoria's reign. Paxton was neither an architect nor an engineer; to begin with, he was a gardener (he wrote a treatise on the dahlia) and an inspired tinkerer. In 1837, a traveler to British Guiana brought back seeds of a large water lily, the sight of which he'd found particularly "refreshing." These seeds were very slow to germinate until Paxton designed a heated tank for them. Within three months the tank was decked with blossoming, raft-like lily pads, five feet in diameter. They were extraordinary enough to send to the Queen and to name after her—*Victoria regia*. One day, Paxton even tried standing his small daughter on one of them, and it easily held her weight. Amazed, he studied the lily's umbrella-like ribs—they were a miracle of economy and strength.

While Paxton turned out to have talent for making railroads, as well as plants, grow large, he didn't forget his water lilies. One after-noon at a committee meeting of the Midland Railway, he started doodling on a blotter. His doodle showed something like an enormous greenhouse supported by iron ribs. These ribs were copied directly from the ribs of his prodigious lily. In time, this sketch would evolve into the plan for the Crystal Palace at the London Exposition (1851). It had an iron framework to carry the weight, so the walls could be completely glass.

Birdcage

Thirty years later, in Chicago, William Le Baron Jenney took the idea one step further. The story goes that one afternoon Jenney came home early from his downtown office. His sudden appearance so startled his wife that she leapt to her feet and dropped the large book she was reading. It landed on a birdcage that for some reason was standing on the floor. While Mrs. Jenney saw to the parrot, William Le Baron stared at the cage: it was undented . . . another miracle of economy and strength. Jenney went on to copy the cage structure in iron for the Home Insurance Building (ten stories), a building generally regarded as the first skyscraper. (The word, by the way, had long been in use for any very tall sail, horse or person, as in "I say, old sky-scraper, is it cold up there?")

Bridge

Then, in 1889, the French government asked Alexandre Gustave Eiffel to whip something up for the Paris Exposition. Eiffel was already famous as a bridge builder, and what he did was to take a bridge-like skeleton and stand it on end: *presto*, a tower. The Eiffel Tower (984 feet—roughly seventy-three stories) easily overtopped the spire of Rouen Cathedral (495 feet), then the tallest in France, but unlike the cathedral, its costs were trifling and its construction incredibly simple. The Eiffel Tower wasn't exactly a building—not yet—but add a few floors and dress the naked thing in brickwork, and why not?

Meanwhile, fortunately for the halt, the overweight, the lazy, and most everyone else, the elevator was developing right along with the steel frame. Elisha Graves Otis of New York developed the first safe model in 1853. In a historic little drama at the New York Crystal Palace, Otis himself stepped onto the platform of his device, which was promptly hauled off the ground by a rope. To the *oohs* and *aahs* of the spectators, dauntless Otis actually cut the hoisting rope. Instead of falling, the elevator merely came to a stop. Otis then said the historical words: "All safe, gentlemen!" Once his safety elevator met the steel frame, the height of future buildings was anyone's guess.

But along with the high tech, the age also turned out its share of doubters of the *If-God-had-meant-us-to-fly - he - would - have - given - us - wings* school of thought, and they were none too enthusiastic about skyscrapers. In 1886 Bradford Lee Gilbert had to badger New York City officials into stretching the Building Code for his newfangled Tower Building (13 stories). Gilbert insisted it would be the safest building in town and he would prove it by occupying the top floors himself. As the skeleton of steel rose, droves of skeptics flocked downtown to watch the fool thing topple. When the framework reached ten stories, the owner of the neighboring building, expecting disaster, sold his property. Finally, a

Sunday morning came when gale winds hit the city, and by the time they were blowing at eighty m.p.h., a huge crowd had assembled—at a safe distance—to see the fun. Then jaunty Mr. Gilbert himself turned up, a piece of string dangling from his pocket and something of a smirk on his face. While the watchmen and janitors from neighboring buildings "were indignant in their outspoken criticisms of him," he blithely

ARDINGHELLI V. SALVUCCI

The Manhattan skyscraper race was not the first. That honor actually belongs to San Gimignano, a lovely little town in the Tuscan hills near Florence which, even today, boasts fourteen or more towers. Back in the 1300's there were fifty or sixty of these tower-houses, some directly across the street from one another.

Charming as San Gimignano is today, the history of those tall towers is far from pleasant. They were in fact fortresses. In the 10th and 11th centuries, blood flowed so freely in the streets of the town the tower houses were the only defense. Two families, the Ardinghelli and the Salvucci, slaughtered each other so savagely that they made the Montagues and the Capulets look like good neighbors.

---

climbed the unfinished skeleton. At the top, with a magician's flourish, he drew from his pocket the string—a plumb line. Then Gilbert slowly lowered the line and let the crowd see for itself. There wasn't the slightest vibration: the building was solid as a rock.

Once Gilbert had cleared the way, the New York skyscraper race was off and running. First came the Flatiron Building (20 stories), then the Times Building (22 stories), then the City Investing Company Building (32 stories), the Singer Building (47 stories) and the Woolworth Building (60 stories). The skyline of New York was turning into a mirror of the whole business world: a battleground of contending giants. And the motives were not strictly financial. Frank Woolworth, for one, plunked down $13 million of his own cash for his tower, knowing perfectly well that his profits would be slim. "Beyond a doubt his ego was a thing of extra size," wrote his builder. "Whoever tried to find a reason for his tall building and did not take that fact into account would reach a false conclusion." Woolworth was a farmer's son from upstate New York, but for his office in "The Cathedral of Commerce" he replicated Napoleon's audience chamber at Compiègne, complete with embossed ceiling, marble wall panels, throne room chairs and bust of Napoleon posing as Caesar.

But this Emperor also liked his little pranks. Before it was completed, Woolworth and his friend Frank Taft went exploring in the tower. Taft pushed on ahead, but the elderly Woolworth scrambled right after him, insisting that no one would out-climb him in his own building. A last ladder brought them right up to the peak. "Say," urged Woolworth, "let's write our names up here." According to Taft: "Both of us then scrawled our names on the rafters and were as much puffed up with pride as though we were youngsters carving our names on a park bench or tree."

The Woolworth was the world's tallest building until the boom year of 1929 when the Bank of Manhattan soared in at seventy-one stories. Then Walter Chrysler, the car whiz, got a little worried about his kids:

> I came to the conclusion that what my boys ought to have was something to be responsible for. They had grown up in New York and probably would want to live there. They wanted to work, and so the idea of putting up a building was born. Something that I had seen in Paris recurred to me. I said to the architects: "Make this building higher than the Eiffel Tower." That was the beginning of the seventy-seven story Chrysler Building.

To keep the competition guessing, Chrysler had his tower finished in an odd way. The steel plates that top it off were hoisted up the outside of the building one at a time and set down in the middle of the sixty-fifth floor. There they were assembled into a spire, which was then suddenly hoisted into place in one twenty-seven-ton piece. It was this last one-hundred-eighty-five-foot burst that made the Chrysler, briefly, the world's champion.

Even as Chrysler's tower was rising, a certain rival from General Motors, John Jacob Raskob, was setting out to top it. And even as

(foreground) film star Marion Marsh (background) the Chrysler Building

Raskob's Empire State Building was being built, an anonymous cigar magnate was publicizing plans for a 1,600 foot, one-hundred-fifty-story colossus. Then the bottom fell out of the stock market, and this first heat of the skyscraper race came to a dead stop.

Chapter 4

HOW TALL CAN YOU BUILD IT SO IT WON'T FALL DOWN?

John Jacob Raskob (left) and Alfred E. Smith cutting up the Waldorf

J

OKE?

Robinson: Raskob? I never heard of Raskob.

Jones: Raskob makes cars go.

Robinson: Oh, I see. Raskob's a kind of lubricating oil!

This knee-slapper was going the rounds back in 1928 when John Jacob Raskob, a vice president at General Motors, popped into office as Democratic National Chairman. Raskob was not exactly a household word. Apart from being unknown, there was another reason why Raskob was an odd choice for Democratic National Chairman—he was a Republican. He was a Republican like almost every other millionaire in the country in those days.

Raskob's wealth was not inherited. When he quit high school to support his family, he scrimped along at $5 a week as stenographer in an Ohio pump concern. In 1902

BEACON LIGHTS

MOORING MECHANISM

OBSERVATION
PLATFORM
ELEVATION 1224 FT.

EXIT FROM
DIRIGIBLE

ENCLOSED
OBSERVATION
LEVEL

ELEVATOR
SHAFT

STAIRS

CABLE TO
WINCHES

LOWER
OBSERVATION
FLOOR

WINCHES
ANCHOR
DIRIGIBLE
TO MAST

*Details of the
dirigible mooring
mast*

William Lamb with (left) two rejected plans for the Empire State Building and (right) the first study of Plan K

he moved over to a street railway company as secretary to the president, Pierre S. duPont. It was a move that changed his life. DuPont's star was on the rise, and Raskob rose right along with him. He was already more protégé than employee when together they helped reorganize E. I. duPont de Nemours and Company. They turned phenomenal profits selling gunpowder during World War I, then bought a controlling interest in G.M. and turned phenomenal profits selling automobiles. Raskob's contribution was to invent the installment plan for buying cars. It made him one of the richer men in the country.

In the late 1920's, Raskob had a second life-changing encounter, this time with Alfred E. ("The Happy Warrior") Smith, four-term governor of New York and Democratic candidate for president. Both men were Catholics and both detested Prohibition. Raskob and Smith liked each other immediately, which Raskob expressed by promptly handing over a check for $50,000. Smith returned the compliment by inviting Raskob to run his campaign. And that's how a Republican became Democratic National Chairman.

Raskob spent hugely in the 1928 campaign against Herbert Hoover. The Democrats sang, "East Side, West Side, all around the town . . ," the Republicans smeared them as the party of "Rum and Romanism," and then November came around. Hoover creamed Smith. The Democrats couldn't even hold the upper South and Texas. The country wasn't ready to see a Catholic in the White House.

Defeated, Smith couldn't offer Raskob a job (he probably would have made him Secretary of the Treasury), but Raskob had one for Smith. Raskob, with Pierre duPont, Pierre's cousin Coleman duPont, and two other financiers, had decided to put up a building in New York. Sensing that Smith, with his immense charm, would make a terrific front man for the project, they hired him at $50,000 a year.

Raskob's original plan for the

Empire State Building was a rather stubby hulk thirty stories high. But just then, the Bank of Manhattan downtown and the Chrysler Building midtown were pushing up the skyscraper records, and the temptation was too much for Raskob. He and Smith might have lost their campaign for president but there was another race they could win. Besides, one acquaintance said, "It burned Raskob to think the French had built something higher than anything we had in this great country of ours." One day the following scene transpired between Raskob and his architect, William Lamb of Shreve, Lamb and Harmon:

John J. finally reached into a drawer and pulled out one of those big fat pencils schoolchildren liked to use. He held it up and he said to Bill Lamb: "Bill, how high can you make it so that it won't fall down?"
—Hamilton Weber,
the original rental manager for the building.

William Lamb couldn't answer right off. In addition to not falling down, the building would also have to turn a profit, conform to the zoning laws, provide adequate light, air, and elevator service, and look beautiful. A fat pencil was a more or less inspiring start, but a scale model it wasn't. Lamb sent his experts out to investigate the technical problems—the steel frame, heating, elevators, ventilating and plumbing. Then he started to draw. Under the 1916 Zoning Law, above the 30th floor, a tower could occupy only one-fourth of the total plot area. With a two acre plot, that meant a half-acre tower. Lamb juggled the huge mass of the building (thirty-six million cubic feet would make it profitable). He shifted the elevator core, carved away setbacks, and continued to draw. It was the sixteenth attempt, Plan K, that finally clicked. Lamb had thrust aside the wedding cake profile favored back then to arrive at clean lines more and more resembling Raskob's original pencil. Lamb made his set-back from the two acre site "in one gorgeous gesture" after the fifth floor. The short, broad base of the building supported a single, sweeping tower, eased by abutments on the way up.

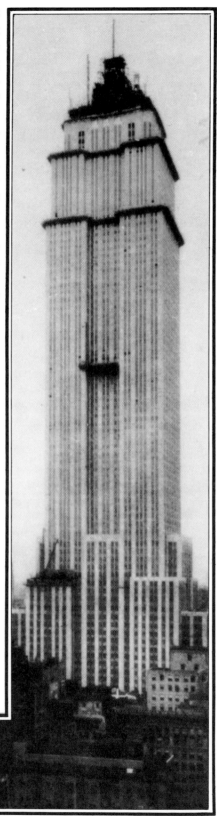

The logic of the plan is very simple. A certain amount of space in the center, arranged as compactly as possible, contains the vertical circulation, toilets, shafts and corridors. Surrounding this is a perimeter of office space 28 feet deep. The sizes of the floors diminish as the elevators decrease in number. In essence, there is a pyramid of nonrentable space surrounded by a greater pyramid of rentable space.
                    –William Lamb

But how tall could they make it so it wouldn't fall down? In the first public announcement, Smith said the height would be "close to 1,000 feet."

We thought we would be the tallest at 80 stories. Then the Chrysler went higher, so we lifted the Empire State to 85 stories, but only four feet taller than the Chrysler. Raskob was wor-

ried that Walter Chrysler would pull a trick—like hiding a rod in the spire and then sticking it up at the last minute.

—Hamilton Weber

At this point, Raskob took a look at a scale model of the eighty-six-story building and said, "It needs a hat!" And for a hat he came up with a suggestion of his own: a dirigible mooring mast towering two hundred feet above the 86th floor. The Graf Zeppelin was already making trans-Atlantic flights, and Raskob saw a way to turn the world's tallest building into the world's most convenient airport too. Smith made the announcement:

The directors of the Empire State, Inc., believe that in a comparatively short time the Zeppelin airships will establish trans-Atlantic, transcontinental and trans-Pacific lines, and possibly a route to South America from the port of New York. Building with an eye to the future, it has been determined to erect this tower to land people directly on Thirty-fourth Street and Fifth Avenue after their ocean trip, seven minutes after the airship connects with the mast.

The top floor of the building would make a perfect international arrival lounge. Although Commander Jerome Hunsaker of the Goodyear Zeppelin Corporation asserted, "This mooring mast is perfectly feasible," plenty of people thought otherwise. "If you know how to hold down the tail of a dirigible," wrote the *New York Telegram*, "former Governor Alfred E. Smith may give you a job." Practicable or not, the mast gave the building a total height of 1,250 feet, a very safe margin over the 1,046-foot Chrysler Building.

The building was not born under a very auspicious star, though.

Demolition on the old Waldorf-Astoria began in October 1929. On October 24, Black Thursday, the Stock Market came tumbling down. Large projects like the Empire State were cut left and right. To back down would mean taking a sure loss; to continue meant risking a still greater loss. Raskob, who had millions in other investments too, urged the American people to buy stock now when prices were depressed. Senator A.R. Robinson swiftly charged him with being "psychologically" responsible for the crash. In December a loan of $27.5 million from the Metropolitan Life Insurance Company gave the Empire State project the extra push it needed. In spite of what people were optimistically terming "the slump," the building would go up.

To sweeten the bitter times, Raskob and his partners were lucky enough to have a small windfall.

The top of the mooring mast

When demolition workers reached the basement level of the Waldorf, they found beneath it a sealed sub-basement that had been covered over when the hotel was built. A padlocked steel door, forced open, gave onto a descending staircase. The room below turned out to be *the* Mrs. Astor's wine cellar, and in it were such goodies as five hogsheads of whiskey dating from the Spanish-American War and more than one hundred cases of choice French wines and champagnes. The partners divided the spoils equally. The rest of the Waldorf-Astoria, some sixteen thousand truckloads of elegant rubble, was dumped at sea five miles off Sandy Hook.

When William Lamb had designed the tallest building in the world, his work was still only half done. Raskob and his partners had a second requirement just as exacting as the height: a construction deadline. They gave Lamb just eighteen months from the start of drawings to the snipping of ribbons on opening day. Any longer delay would tie up their $50 million investment too long without profits. The building would have to rise at an incredible speed. To achieve this, Lamb did away with hand work wherever possible. Glass, stone and steel parts were designed for accurate mass production and simple assembly. Marble for the lobby and corridors was chosen for quick delivery. Furthermore, Lamb and his partners devised a new technique for attaching windows. Instead of being set back in stone frames, the glass was applied directly to the outer walls of the building with light metal brackets. Vertical metal strips connected window to window all the way up the building, and aluminum spandrels filled in the

spaces. This gave the whole building a gleaming, streamlined effect at the same time that it yielded more floor space and halved the stone work.

Starrett Brothers and Eken, the builders, mapped out their construction strategy in minute detail. An overlapping schedule would coordinate the various stages of the job: demolition—October 1929 to February 1930; excavation—January to March; structural steel—March to September; exterior masonry—June to December; metal window frames—May to January 1931, elevators and mail chutes—May to February, etc.

Excavation for the foundations went no deeper than thirty-five feet. Even so, the rock and earth removed from the site weighed almost as much as the finished building would. The timid were reassured that the weight of the Empire State Building would be so evenly distributed that no square inch of the site would bear more pressure than a "French heel." Excavation went on twenty-four hours a day and foundations were laid on one side of the site even as the steam shovels were still digging out the other.

Next came the steel frame. Steel poured into H-beams and I-beams in Pittsburgh was rushed to a supply depot in New Jersey, ferried across the Hudson by barge, trucked to 34th and Fifth and lifted into place by nine powerful electric derricks. Total time: eighty hours. Then the high-iron gang fitted up the steel by bolting and the riveting gang came through to finish the job. The heater would toast each rivet on a small stove and tong it thirty feet to the catcher, who fielded it in his bucket and offered it to the bucker-up, who bucked it into the hole. Then the

*Empire State
Building construction
photos by Lewis Hine
(through page 37)*

riveter, with his gun, came around the opposite side to flatten its nose. This infield in the sky rose higher and higher with the steel until it was playing catch 1,000 feet above Fifth Avenue. Raskob's "hat" went on in January 1931 in spite of fierce north winds with freezing rain and fog. The whole skeleton took 57,000 tons of steel, three times as much as the Chrysler Building, and enough to lay a double railroad track to Baltimore.

Lewis Hine, the photographer, followed the three hundred steel-workers up into the sky. Their fearlessness and concentration gave Hine "a new zest of high adventure" and inspired a magnificent series of pictures. Hine celebrated the "sky boys who ride the ball to the 90th floor or higher, and defy death to the staccato chattering of a pneumatic riveting-hammer." He did some death defying himself: some shots required him to swing out from the building in a specially designed basket.

To speed construction after the steelwork, building supplies were not delivered by wheelbarrow but by a temporary railway adapted to coordinate with the elevators.

On each floor, as the steel frame climbed higher, a miniature railroad was built, with switches and cars, to carry supplies. A perfect time-table was published each morning. At every minute of the day the builders knew what was going up on each of the elevators, to which height it would rise, and which gang of workers would use it. On each floor, the operators of every one of the small trains of cars knew what was coming up and where it would be needed.

Trucks did not wait, derricks and elevators did not swing idle, men did not wait.

37

—Empire State, A Short History, 1931

Stairways, electrical cables, plumbing, concrete floor arches and outer walls followed directly after the steelwork. The speed gave *The New York Times* the impression of a "chase up into the sky." During the spring and summer of 1930, some 3,400 workers were in the chase, installing 6,700 radiators, fifty-one miles of pipes, seventeen million feet of telephone cable, seven miles of elevator shafts, and a ventilating system capable of pulling one million cubic feet of fresh air into the building every minute. During one ten day period in the fall, the building jumped a total of fourteen floors. The time pressure may have been one cause of accidents on the job: fourteen lives were lost during construction, as compared to just one on the Chrysler Building. Buckminster Fuller suggested that these lives might have been spared if Empire State had been built horizontally and then hoisted upright.

In spite of the speed, standards of work remained very high. John Crowley, a carpenter on the job, still remembers: "You had to turn out a perfect job there—the tenants looked for it, and they got it!" He remembers how the concrete floors were first poured: "They were perfectly square and perfectly plumb—like a beautiful piece of glass." He also remembers John Jacob Raskob stopping by to smoke a pipe. "Raskob was the most democratic man anybody could want to see. Money didn't change him— he'd talk to anybody, he wouldn't pass anybody up." Naturally, Crowley loves the building. As he says, in a brogue untainted by a lifetime in America, "It's a doll, it's a prin*cess*, it stands alone for good lines."

As the building reached completion in the spring of 1931, it was clear that it would break several kinds of construction records. The steel was topped out twelve days ahead of schedule, the exterior limestone thirteen days ahead. In fact, the tallest building in the world went up in just one year and forty-five days. Furthermore, thanks to the Depression, it came in under cost: at about $41 million, instead of the estimated $50 million.

Sidewalk superintendents who had been watching since the first excavation could finally see just how the Empire State would look. The design was clearly Art Deco, the going style for skyscrapers, but a pretty modest version of it. Art Deco, originally a French import, offered a sumptuous, popular version of urban chic. Where, after World War II, the International Style would pare down form to a functional minimum (giving us glass and steel boxes), Art Deco gave birth to skyscrapers that were exuberant, entertaining and theatrical as well as businesslike. Empire State's chief rival, the Chrysler Building, went to flamboyant extremes—from the gleaming metallic scales of the finial tower, to the gargoyles, winged radiator caps and frieze of mudguards along the shaft, to the dazzling hardwood veneers and brilliant colors of the triangular lobby.

Compared to such racy versions of Art Deco, the Empire State is a model of restraint. Architect William Lamb had a reputation for soberness (he frowned on Grand Central Station as the "Little Nemo school of architecture"), and for the

Metal bridge in the Empire State Building lobby

To Frances Lamport
with best wishes   [signature]

Al Smith and friends at the opening day radio broadcast from the 86th floor

exterior of the Empire State he simply used the vertical window lines to emphasize what the building already had in great abundance: height. Decorative touches were restricted to the aluminum spandrels connecting the windows, the grand entrances (the one on Fifth Avenue flanked by a pair of very modest lions) and the streamlined, futuristic modeling of the dirigible mast. Even the mast, the most extravagant

touch, could theoretically pass as functional. The lobby, with its splendid relief of the Empire State Building and its handsome metal bridges, was a bit more lavish, but still restrained.

The press, while commenting on the disparity between the high of the building and the low of the economy, generally extolled the Empire State as "building in excelsis" and "poetry in steel." One

staffer for the *New Republic*, though, was troubled by what he saw as one more step in the dehumanizing of New York. Still, even he found something to enjoy: an anonymous electrician or plasterer had added his own humanizing touch to the 55th floor—a mural in pencil.

A large male figure is seen standing upright and fornicating, Venus aversa, with a stooping female fig-

Opening day

LET THERE BE LIGHT

In a negative way, the shape of the Empire State Building, owes a great deal to the Equitable Building, erected in 1915 at 120 Broadway. The Equitable still stands today, and it is still overbearing. It rises forty stories straight up from an entire city block, and, as one early critic put it, it "throws a shadow that covers seven-and-a-half acres at noon on the 21st of December." The Equitable hogs a whole neighborhood's supply of light and air, and when it first opened, its 1.4 million square feet of office space drained the nearby buildings of tenants.

In 1916, New York City responded to the Equitable Building with its first attempt to regulate the skyscraper free-for-all—the 1916 Zoning Law. The law ruled that a tower could not rise straight up from an entire building site. Beyond a certain height, buildings had to be set back from the sidewalk line at a designated angle—hence the step-like shape of so many New York skyscrapers, which, in obedience to the law, receded from the sidewalk in a series of set-backs. This guaranteed at least a minimum of light and air to the rest of the neighborhood.

---

ure, who has no arms but pendulous breasts. The man is saying, "O, man!" One is grateful to the man who drew [this picture]. He has done something to take the curse off the opening of the Empire State Building.

Cursed or not, opening day, May 1, 1931, dawned brilliantly clear. Two of Al Smith's grandchildren cut a ribbon at the Fifth Avenue entrance; President Hoover, in Washington, pressed a button that lit up the tower; and Governor Franklin D. Roosevelt saluted the vision and faith of the builders. Flashy Mayor Jimmy Walker (he drove a $17,000 Dusenberg), whose administration was undergoing far-reaching investigations for corruption, then thanked the builders for providing "a place higher, further removed than any in the world, where some public official might like to come and hide." And Smith read a telegram from William Lamb, already relaxing on a sea voyage: "One day out," he wired, "and I can still see the building!"

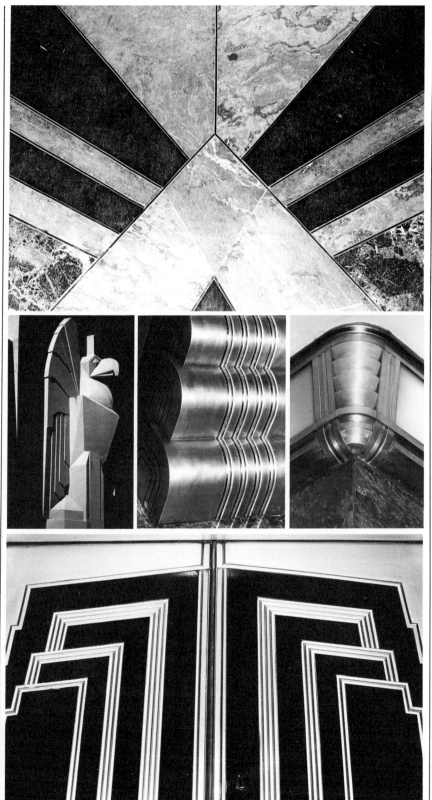

THE EMPTY STATE BUILDING

E*mpire State seemed almost to float, like an enchanted fairy tower, over New York. An edifice so lofty, so serene, so marvelously simple, so luminously beautiful, had never before been imagined. One could look back on a dream well planned.* —Empire State, A Short History, 1931

In some ways, the dream *was* miraculously well planned. The design promptly won awards for Shreve, Lamb and Harmon from the New York Architectural League and the New York chapter of the American Institute of Architects. The president of the latter said, "The noble simplicity of this outstanding structure makes it an inspiring landmark in our city."

It would take somewhat longer to judge the engineering achievement. In order to minimize vibrations, Empire State's steel skeleton was designed to give slightly before high winds. In the early days, feature writers liked to exaggerate this effect, giving the public some wild ideas. A boy from Oklahoma once wrote, "My pal Terry and I have a bet. He says she sways thirty-eight feet in the wind, but I say it's fifty feet. Which is right?" The precise answer wasn't at hand until 1956, when aeronautical engineers from Minneapolis-Honeywell installed an ultra-precise gyroscope on the 85th floor. They proved that in a high wind the Empire State shifts no more than one-quarter inch off center. Thay means a total sway of one-half inch, tiny enough to solidify the building's reputation as an engineering masterpiece. (Still, in winds over twenty m.p.h., up on the 66th floor the delicate scales in the Empire Diamond Corporation go haywire, swinging as much as fifteen points. At $50 a point, those are expensive vibrations.)

Other aspects of the dream were not so perfectly planned—the dirigible mast, for one. In September 1931 a small dirigible managed to tie up to the mast for a total of three minutes. No one had fully reckoned on the updraft caused by a 40 m.p.h. wind slapping aginst such a tall structure. Two weeks later, when the Navy blimp Columbia made the same attempt, the buffeting nearly upended it. To right the blimp, the captain released some of his water ballast, which fell several blocks away. Pedestrians there were soaked by a sudden cloudburst

out of a perfectly clear sky. Meanwhile, the blimp very nearly yanked workers and celebrities right off the tower. Finally, it dropped bundles of *The New York Evening Journal* onto the observation deck, and they were retrieved by a workman held at the ankles by John Jacob Raskob himself. As far as dirigibles were concerned, the mast was a flop. The top of it, though, converted to a second observation deck, soon offered visitors a vast panorama from the 102nd story.

But blimps were a minor problem. The Depression had zapped the real estate market before Raskob, Smith and company could deliver their two million square feet of new office space. Finding tenants was a major problem. While Raskob had originally pictured the building as home for blue-chip companies, Hamilton Weber, the renting manager, had to set his sights lower. Huge ads featuring pictures of the Astor mansions and the Waldorf-Astoria went on about "the world's most distinguished address," but Empire State was only forty-six percent rented when it opened in 1931, and only sixty-eight percent rented in the succeeding years. Many of the early tenants were textile and notions companies, later joined by hosiery, lingerie and shoe concerns. Raskob tried unsuccessfully to bring the carpet industry into the building, and Smith found himself pleading for tax breaks because the building was partially unoccupied. In the Depression years Smith's own politics swerved sharply to the right, but in spite of his tirades against the "socialistic bureaucrats indulging in communistic planning and crackpot reforms" (the New Deal), Smith had to make a humiliating pilgrimage to Washington to ask FDR's help in renting space to the Department of Commerce.

Vaudeville entertainers spoofed the building's woes with routines about "The Empty State Building," "The 102-Story Blunder" and "Smith's Folly." One real estate man opined that the only way to fill it was to tow it out to sea. Oddly enough, the last word on this subject went to the King of Siam. Al Smith was showing the building to King Prajadhipok and Queen Rambhai Barni when the king suddenly said, "This reminds me of home."

"Why?" asked Smith. "You don't have anything like this in Siam."

"Oh yes," quipped the monarch, "we have white elephants, too."

If the owners were perplexed about what to do with the building, there were plenty of people around who weren't. In February 1932 the Polish Olympic ski team tried to launch a new sport when they raced up the 1,860 steps to the top in just twenty-one minutes. On the 102nd floor they met the Czech ski team, which had just beaten them at Lake Placid. The Czechs challenged the Poles to a staircase race. At this point the management of Empire State stepped in and squelched the event—they weren't interested in causing coronaries.

The Poles were left with the title until 1978 when the New York Road Runner's Club revived the sport. The building's management smiled on the idea this time, partly because entrance, by invitation, was limited to runners who had completed an ultramarathon (31 miles). Gary Muhrcke, 37, won the first running in 12 minutes, 32.7 seconds. ("It was a kind of sprint," he said.) The day was beautiful and, never having been to the Empire State, Gary wanted to see the view. The sights were just fine, but Muhrcke's victory caused a small storm when the newspapers discovered that he was getting an $11,822-a-year disability pension from the Fire Department. Doctors who reviewed his case decided that nothing was amiss—Muhrcke could run, but he couldn't lift weight.

Back in the building's early days, the owners nixed suggestions by Douglas Leigh, creator of spectacular billboards near Times Square, to turn the top into a giant Coke bottle or a glowing cigarette. The same answer went to human flies who offered to climb up the front of the building and highwire artists who wanted to walk a tightrope to the Chrysler Building up on 42nd Street.

The management did prove receptive to more dignified proposals. In the early 1930's, GE and RCA mounted an experimental television antenna on the building from which they successfully broadcast images of Mickey Mouse and Felix the Cat. GE also erected a sixty-foot rod to help in its studies of lightning. For several summers a young engineer was quartered in a nearby hotel. When thunderheads approached the city, he dashed over to Empire State, took the elevators as far as they went, and climbed to a roost up in the attic. There he switched on his instruments and waited for 100,000-volt lightning bolts to blast the rod. A cohort in another building simultaneously photographed each flash. They found the rod repeatedly jolted by 200,000 amps of electricity, sometimes as often as nine times in twenty minutes. Of course, the building's steel skeleton conducts the current harmlessly into the earth. The static electric build-up is so mammoth, though, that under the right conditions, if you stick your hand through the observatory fence, St. Elmo's fire will stream from your fingertips. Lovers who kiss up there may find their lips crackling with electric sparks.

In 1947 the management of Empire State installed "the most powerful musical instrument in the world"—a set of gargantuan carillon bells—in the tower. The contraption pumped Christmas carols out onto the breeze. They couldn't be heard in the streets directly below, but some people did hear them come wafting in near Coney Island, sixteen miles away, and Hoboken. Over at Times Square, Police Lieutenant Daniel Kearns said the music was drowned out by the traffic. Anyway, he went on, "It would take more than bells to excite anybody here in Times Square."

Gary Muhrcke taking the 1978 staircase race

A PORTFOLIO

Pierre Le Tan

Eugene Mihaesco

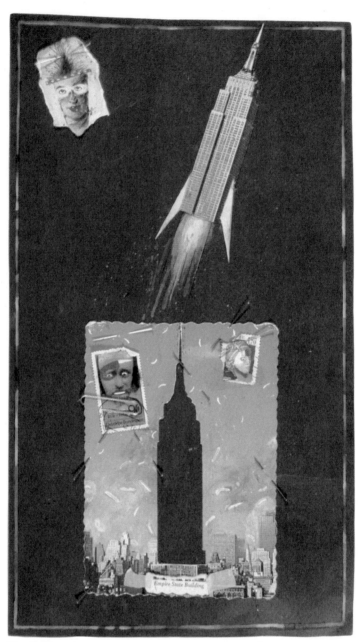

Henrik Drescher

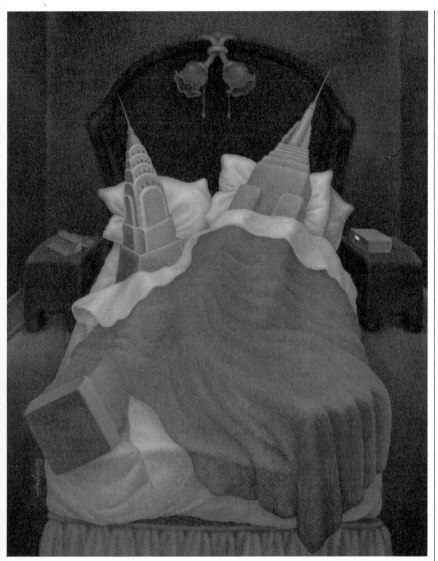

Robert Goldstrum

Paul Degen

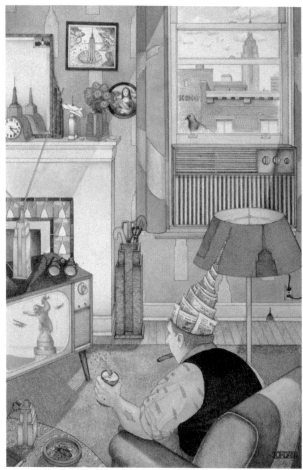

Craig Jordan

Andrej Dudzinski

Randall Enos

56

Chapter 6

CLIMB
YOU FOOL
CLIMB

In circle and on facing page: damage from the 1945 bomber crash

WAR BONDS

59

MIRACLE O

Gust of wind saves woman who leaped from 86th floor of Empire State Buildin

By SAM ROSENSOHN

OFFICIALS said today it was miraculous that a woman who jumped last night from the 86th floor observation deck of the ~~Empire State Building sur-~~

skyscraper recalled th Hawaiian man leaped the same observation about a year ago and blown back to the floor.

Police said the we ~~~~ say why she

in such a hard thing o Id.

not believe else on t leck whe ence.

is were s Ir so col e who wa city last e enclosed ck on th

Observatory manager with dead birds

landed on the ledge directly below.

Her only injury was a fractured pelvis, according to Bellevue Hospital.

She was discovered at 8:20 p.m., when security guard Frank Clark heard a woman moaning in pain.

He looked out of an 85th floor office window and saw Miss Adams lying on the concrete ledge.

New York Post story on Elvita Adams, December 3, 1979

Tourists (unsuccessfully) begging Ronald Ravitz not to jump

The Depression was only the start of Empire State's bad luck. Tremendous height turned out to be a mixed blessing in small ways as well as large. The building, for example, invaded the flyways of migrating birds, which were confused by its lights on foggy nights. One murky night in 1948, hundreds of warblers and red-eyed vireos crashed into the tower, and their bodies rained down onto the set-backs and sidewalks. Pedestrians below gathered up the survivors and tried to restore their strength with food from nearby restaurants. Since then the floodlights on the tower have been turned off during foggy nights of the spring and fall migration seasons.

But the bodies that fell accidentally were a minor problem compared to the ones that fell on purpose. A structure so tall and so famous inevitably became a magnet to the desperate and the crazed. Even before the Empire State was finished, a discharged worker had hurled himself down an open elevator shaft, and it was just eighteen months after opening day that the building had its next suicide.

As they rode the small elevator

Reprinted by permission of the New York Post. © 1979, New York Post Corporation.

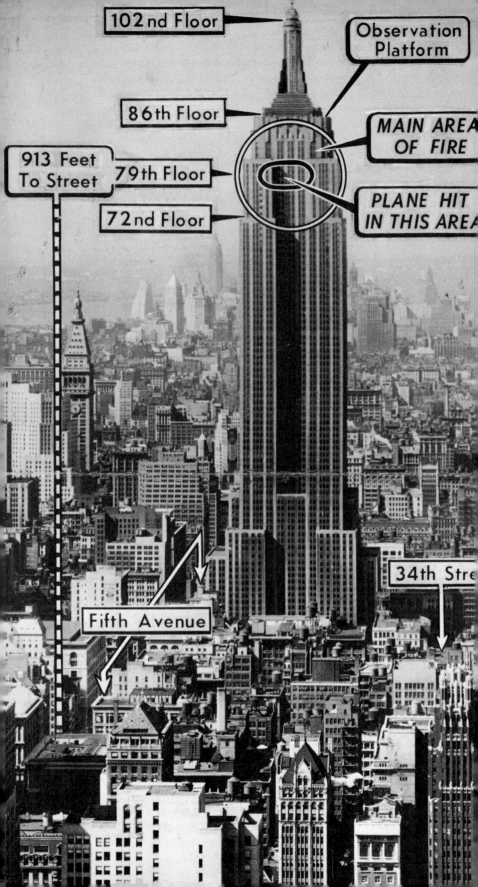

102 nd Floor

Observation Platform

86th Floor

MAIN AREA OF FIRE

913 Feet To Street

79th Floor

72nd Floor

PLANE HIT IN THIS AREA

Fifth Avenue

34th Stre

from the 86th floor to the 102nd, Pierrepont Stackpole of Boston noticed that his fellow-passenger was extraordinarily nervous. The man's blue eyes were wild, and he continually fidgeted with five cigars he had in a package. When the door opened on 102, the man quickly hurdled an iron gate and ran up a staircase leading to an open platform at the 103rd story that was intended for dirigible passengers. Before Stackpole or the guard on duty could catch him the man jumped. His body crashed onto a setback at the 87th floor and rolled onto the roof of the 86th. No wallet was found on his body but in one pocket there was a photograph of several German schoolboys standing with a priest, and under it, in German, the words: "My darling: this is a picture of my son Arnim, which was taken in Astoria, Long Island." The next day, the man was positively identified as Friedrich Eckert, thirty-three, a storekeeper from Queens.

Friedrich Eckert was only the first. Although the guards and ticket-sellers kept watch for despondent and solitary types, a total of sixteen people would make the leap before the guard rail was finally raised. In one three-week period in 1947, vigilant guards hauled five jumpers back from the edge. The present fence, finally erected that year, has cut down the numbers. The stone wall is now surmounted by wire mesh and then incurving steel spikes that rise seven feet off the floor. Still, a really determined person can make it over. One of the oddest cases of all was Elvita Adams, who did just that on the cold night of December 2, 1979. She jumped from the 86th floor observatory, but a strong gust of wind promptly blew her right back to the building. She landed on a two-and-a-half foot ledge at the 85th story, fracturing her hip. A guard who heard her moaning then pulled her through a window to safety.

The grip of the Depression had just about loosened on Empire State, and the empty upper floors were quickly filling with tenants when the building met its darkest day, July 28, 1945, a day that has burned itself into New Yorkers' memories with some of the same vividness as Pearl Harbor Day. On that Saturday morning, an Army B-25 bomber crashed into the north face of the Empire State, killing fourteen people and injuring twenty-six.

Lieutenant Colonel William Smith, the pilot, highly decorated for more than five hundred hours of combat duty in Europe, had recently returned to the states. The European war was over, and Smith was due for transfer to the Pacific. On that rainy morning he received orders to fly the B-25 from Bedford Field, near Boston, down to Newark Airport to pick up his commanding officer. Newark Airport is just across the Hudson, south and west of Manhattan, but after an uneventful flight, Smith turned up instead at LaGuardia Airport, east of Manhattan. There he requested the weather report for Newark. Visibility over New York was very poor, and the LaGuardia tower considered landing him right where he was. But the military authorities had a slightly better reading of the Newark weather, and in the end Smith was given permission to proceed to Newark as long as he had three miles of forward visibility. When the War Department later investigated the crash, they judged the tower wrong in clearing Smith for Newark and Smith wrong in flying over Manhattan in such foul weather. The last transmission from the tower to Smith was ominous: "From where I'm sitting, I can't see the top of the Empire State Building."

In the tragedy that followed mechanical trouble and poor judgment may both have played their part. Smith's course took him right across Manhattan, where his altitude should have been over 2,000 feet. Instead, he came in low enough to rattle windowpanes and turn heads all over midtown. The towers of the city were shrouded in swirling fog and clouds. Smith was crossing Manhattan roughly on the level of 42nd Street, which put him dangerously close to the office tower above Grand Central Station. Vincent Galbo saw the plane no higher

New York City firemen with man rescued from 79th floor

Remains of a propeller

than the 22nd floor as it neared the building. Smith banked to avoid it, but that put him on a collision course with the 700 foot Salmon Tower. Smith had survived flak and attacking Messerschmitts, but now, traveling at more than 200 m.p.h., he was caught in the maze of New York skyscrapers. Further, some witnesses insist, he was having rudder trouble. They watched in horror as the bomber banked and weaved

overhead. Stan Lomax, a sports announcer for WOR radio, found himself shouting, "Climb, you fool, climb!" By then the B-25 was heading straight for the Empire State. At the last moment, the plane seemed to lunge upward, but it was too late. At 9:50 a.m. the twelve-ton bomber smashed into the 79th floor. Watchers in the street saw the tower suddenly flash out of the mist as the gas tanks exploded, sending orange flames up to the 86th floor. The wings sheared off, and one engine flew across the 78th floor, smashing through the south wall and landing on a roof across 33rd Street. The other engine and part of a landing gear tore down an elevator shaft into the sub-basement. Eight hundred gallons of flaming gasoline poured down stairways and halls as far as the 75th floor, filling the air with choking fumes. Debris and glass

Debris from crash in street

fell blocks away, while a large piece of the plane stayed wedged in the eighteen-by-twenty-foot hole it had blasted in the building.

War was very much on people's minds (American troops were battling for Guam just then) and some who saw the crash from afar guessed it was a Japanese kamikaze attack. One man inside the Empire State who had spent many years in China assumed it was an earthquake: the whole building moved twice, then settled. Merwin Hart, on the 75th floor, thought it was going to fall apart.

Fortunately, it was a foggy Saturday morning, and there were few people in offices or on the observation deck. But the 79th floor *was* occupied. It housed the Catholic War Relief Services, and several workers were at their desks. One was Catherine O'Connor.

The plane exploded within the building. There were five or six seconds—I was tottering on my feet trying to keep my balance— and three-quarters of the office was instantaneously consumed in this sheet of flame. One

man was standing inside the flame. I could see him. It was a co-worker, Joe Fountain. His whole body was on fire. I kept calling to him, "Come on, Joe; come on, Joe." He walked out of it.

Joe Fountain would die of his injuries four days later. Miss O'Connor and a handful of other survivors made their way to a small room on the 33rd Street side of the floor. They had just seen the three men in the plane and ten co-workers incinerated, and they themselves were completely surrounded by flames and pitch-black smoke. Far off, in another part of the building, they watched a man talking on the telephone. There was no way to catch his eye. There was little hope of surviving. According to Miss O'Connor, they prayed.

When firemen and volunteers finally reached this small knot of survivors, they were shocked to find anyone still alive. It was Donald Molony who brought Catherine O'Connor downstairs. "He was the cutest thing. He picked me up in his arms and carried me," she later said.

Crash damage being surveyed

67

She was not the first person Molony rescued that day. Then seventeen, Molony was on leave from a Coast Guard medical training program. Sightseeing in New York, he was debating whether or not to hang around the Empire State Building until the weather cleared so he could go up the tower. Then came the crash.

Being very young and inexperienced I headed for the trouble. There was a drug store on the ground floor of the building. Somehow I talked them into giving me some morphine, syringes, and other first aid supplies. Seeing the red cross on my uniform, one of the firemen grabbed me by the arm and we headed for the basement.

They headed down rather than up because that's where they'd just heard two elevators crash. One engine of the B-25, in its flaming flight through the building, had smashed through the brick-walled elevator shafts, shearing an I-beam. Betty Lou Oliver, a 20-year-old elevator operator, was just descending from the 79th floor when her car began to fall. Automatic safety devices slowed the elevator somewhat, but it still gathered speed as it continued to fall, and when it landed, it hit with enough force for the rubber bumper at the bottom of the shaft to thrust right through the floor. Meanwhile, from above, heavy loops of cable came tumbling down. Still, miraculously, after a seventy-six-story fall, Betty Lou Oliver was alive under the cables. Donald Molony was small enough to slip through a hole in the roof of her elevator. When he reached Mrs. Oliver, she whispered, "Thank God the Navy's here." He helped see that she was safely removed from the elevator before dashing up-

stairs to continue his heroics. Mrs. Oliver spent the next eighteen weeks in Bellevue Hospital recovering from a broken back and legs. She and her husband later returned to Fort Smith, Arkansas, where they opened a grocery store and raised three children. Molony, who would be decorated by the city and the Navy for his courage that day, later went on to distinguish himself as a hospital corpsman in Korea.

Many of those who survived the disaster would carry the damage from burns and smoke inhalation for the rest of their lives. Still, the toll was not nearly as high as it might have been. Up on the observation deck, in spite of the heat, smoke and debris, the waltz music never stopped, and manager Frank Powell was able to lead the fifty or sixty sightseers down to safety. Although the elevators could bring firemen only as high as the 67th floor and they then had to plod up eleven or twelve flights of stairs carrying heavy hoses, they brought the gasoline fire under control in forty minutes. Meanwhile, one trio in an office survived because they were resourceful enough to break a hole in a wall with a small hammer and drag themselves to safety. Perhaps the luckiest of all were Jack McCloskey and Edmund Cummings, two Catholic Relief staffers who, earlier that morning, had been standing very near the spot where the plane entered the building. At 9:30 A.M. their director had phoned to have them meet him in the barber shop instead of in the office. They reached the rendezvous downstairs just as the plane hit up above.

And the building itself survived. The bomber's impact bent one steel beam inward a good eighteen inches, but neither that, nor the

Crash damage under repair

gallons of flaming gasoline, nor the gallons of firefighters' water did any harm to the overall structure. One year and a million dollars later, and the Empire State Building was as good as new.

Repairs were barely underway when trouble struck again—this time in much milder form. On September 24, 1945 the elevator operators went out on strike, stranding the Empire State Building, along with 2,000 other skyscrapers. Some executives tried to set up shop in the lobby, giving dictation and sending secretaries to phone booths to place calls. Up on the 85th floor, the NBC television engineers were prepared: they'd provided themselves with cots and a refrigerator full of food. Below, on the 68th floor, one tenant was expecting a very important phone call, so he waited in his office for it to come. He was there three days later when it did. Food was a problem for anyone who did make the hike to work. One luncheonette operator lugged one hundred fifty sandwiches and several jugs of coffee all the way to the 31st floor. The famished stock brokers up there rewarded him with a $75 tip.

Chapter 7

GIVES AN IMPRESSION OF HEIGHT DOESN'T IT?

Kata Ragosa, King of Morova in the Solomon Islands

The Depression, the bomber and the strikes notwithstanding, in one respect the Empire State Building was always healthy: as a tourist attraction. The tallest building in the world was instantly a must for every visitor to New York. After all, the observatory was "as high as you can get without actually flying." On opening day, back in 1931, the crowds got their first glimpse:

> *Few failed to exclaim at the smallness of man and his handiwork as seen from this great distance. They saw men and motor cars creeping like insects through the streets; they saw elevated trains that looked like toys.*
>
> —The New York Times

Al Smith with Winston Churchill

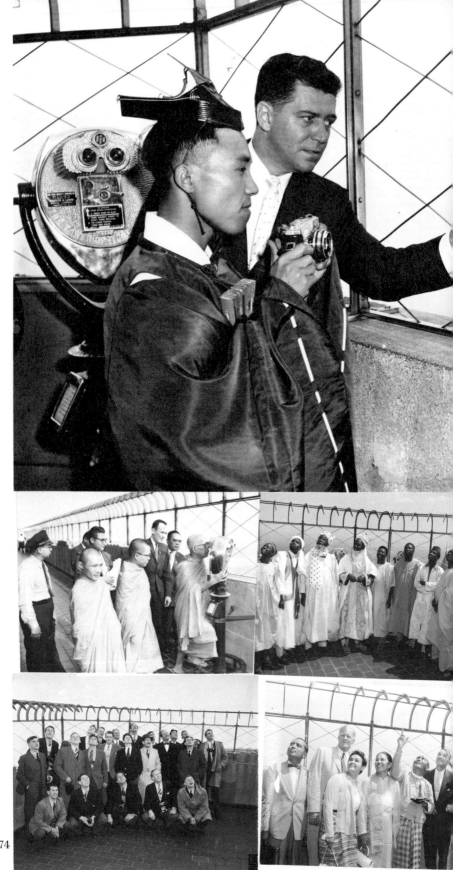

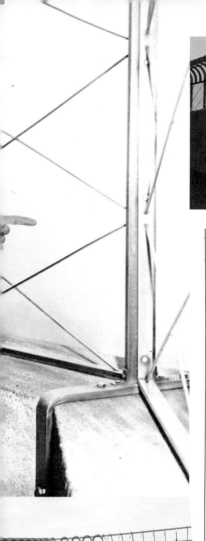

In theory, on a clear day the visibility should be eighty miles, but haze rarely makes that possible. Still, Patchogue, Long Island and Bridgeport, Connecticut are visible, especially with the help of the pay-as-you-look telescopes.

The original observatory was quite an elegant affair. The soda fountain was a stunning Art Deco piece made of black Belgian marble, the West Lounge provided plush wicker chairs for viewing the sunset, and the Café served no fewer than five varieties of French champagne. All this has since given way to food machines, pizza and hot dogs.

Smith kept the building in the news by inviting the great, the near-great and the not-so-great for personal tours. The only man known to have refused his invitation was Walter Chrysler. Newspapers around the world printed photos of Smith

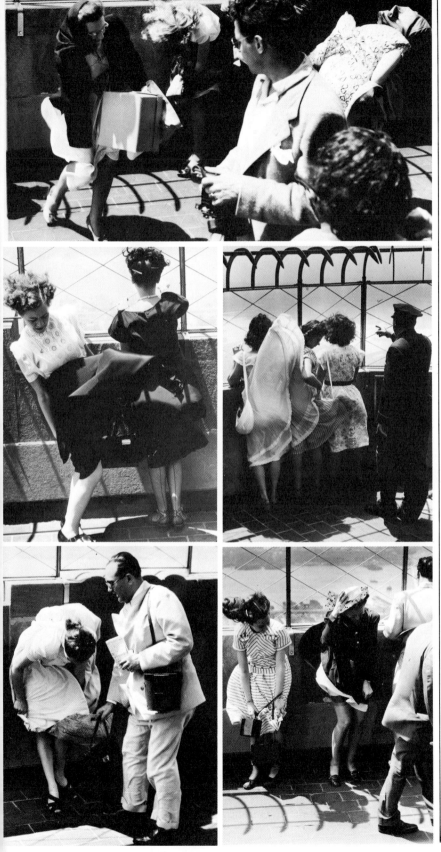

doing the honors for French Premier Pierre Laval and family, Japanese Prince Chichibu, Mr. and Mrs. Anthony Eden, the three pretty sisters of King Zog of Albania (who insisted they were not in America to find rich husbands), Vittorio Mussolini (Il Duce's son) and Archduke Otto von Hapsburg, pretender to the Austrian throne. Then there were shots of Smith looking up through a telescope at Robert Wadlow, the world's tallest man (8'7") and, year after year, with his grin never diminishing, Smith exchanging his brown derby for the Stetson worn by

*Fidel Castro's visit
on April 23, 1959*

some pretty cowgirl from Texas. Other VIP's over the years included Albert Einstein, George Bernard Shaw, H.G. Wells ("It was a great show"), Winston Churchill, Pope Pius XII, Nikita Khrushchev, Fidel Castro and Queen Elizabeth II (She said, "It's beautiful, it's beautiful!")

Winston Churchill, as a matter of fact, was knocked down by a New York taxi just a few days after visiting the building. Al Smith rushed to his hospital room (Smith pronounced the word *horspital)* and demanded to be left alone with Churchill. "I suppose you think of

Miss Teen Queen

me as a politician," said Smith, "but just now I am a diagnostician, and I have brought you a little medicine." From his hip pocket, Smith produced a bottle of Scotch.

Another Smith legend has him encountering a fearful old lady just stepping into one of the express elevators to the top of the Empire State. The lady looked apprehensively at the controls, and then looked up at Smith. "Governor," she quavered, "if something goes wrong, will I go up or down?"

"That," Smith replied, "all de-

pends on what kind of life you've led."

In the early days, the Empire State observatory was the chic spot to shoot fashion ads, launch charity drives, release helium balloons and photograph beauty contestants. It served other purposes too. In 1938, Abdul Assan and the Shogola Olaba dancers from the Congo thought the observatory's great height would assist their ritual to dispel some evil spirits cursing their theatrical engagement (results: unknown). In April 1932, Doris Welchans and

im for Health queen contest

(Clockwise from upper left) Joy Lansing, Nikita Khrushchev, Gina Lollobrigida, President Diem of South Vietnam, Archbishop Makarios

William Holmes were married in the observatory. In 1934 it was the scene of a famous tryst. Tilly Losch, the Viennese dancer, was married to Edward F.W. James. But according to charges he made at their divorce trial, Miss Losch had a secret rendezvous with the dashing Prince Serge Obolensky. The site: the Empire State Building observatory. The tryst continued in the back of a New York taxi, where, the evidence read, the two managed a kiss that lasted fifty blocks.

Less-famous visitors to the building came in droves. In the Depression years they contributed largely to the building's income, and they also bought souvenirs by the millions: replicas of the Empire State in all sizes, water globes with snow, candles, pencil sharpeners, powder boxes, lamps and posters. In 1976 the fifty-millionth visitor stepped out of the elevator, Helga Eilers of Germany. She and her husband Ingo received an official key to New York, a lifetime pass to the observatory, a silver desk model of the Empire State, a Steuben glass Big Apple, a week's stay at the St. Moritz Hotel and a refund on their $1.70 tickets (the city still kept its 13-cent sales tax). Currently, visitors are flooding in at a rate of one and a half million a year. The World Trade Center has not hurt business at all.

One of the people most impressed by the tower could not see at all—Helen Keller. She wrote her impressions after the visit:

> Standing there 'twixt earth and sky, I saw a romantic edifice wrought by human brains and hands that is to the burning eye of the sun a rival luminary. I saw it stand erect and serene in the midst of storm and tumult of elemental commotion. I heard the hammer of Thor ring when the shaft began to rise upward. I saw the unconquerable steel, the flash of testing flames, the swordlike rivets. I heard the steel drills in pandemonium. I saw countless skilled workers welding together that mighty symmetry. I looked upon the marvel of frail yet indomitable hands that lifted the Tower to its dominating height.

> Let cynics and supersensitive souls say what they will about American materialism and machine civilization. Beneath the surface are poetry, mysticism and inspiration that the Empire Building somehow symbolizes. In that giant shaft I see a groping toward beauty and spiritual vision. I am one of those who see and yet believe.

A British chap who visited the observatory in the early days was less effusive: "Gives an impression 84 of height, doesn't it?" he said.

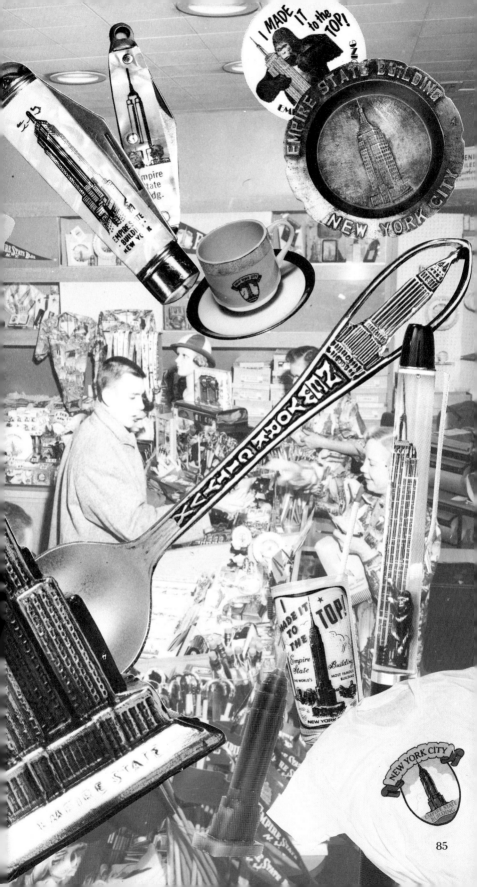

THE WORLD'S LARGEST CHRISTMAS TREE

The appearance of the Empire State has changed three times since the building first opened. A fourth proposed change, the most radical of all, will probably never take place.

Right from the start, the history

*Erecting the
master television
antenna*

of the building was intertwined with the history of television. In 1950, the building grew another two hundred twenty-two feet when a master television antenna was riveted in place atop the dirigible mast. The antenna improved reception for all major channels in the city and raised the building's height to 1,472 feet. With a fifty-two mile broadcast range it reached one-tenth of the people then living in the United States. The sixty ton steel addition had to sit on a base no larger than a pitcher's mound. Its construction was interrupted at one point by a bombardment of tiny pellets that forced the steelworkers down to safety. Scientists called in to check found that the men had been pelted with a peck of barley blown all the way from the Middle West. Today, a newer, taller antenna on the World Trade Center is offering serious competition to Empire State's.

In 1962, the building got its first washing. Thirty men, working from baskets suspended from the top, took six months to scrub down the 500,000 square feet of limestone facade and restore it to its original grey color. All the scrubbers were experienced at high altitudes and one was a former Marine paratrooper. The job cost $200,000, but the insurance policy covering possible accidents during the cleaning was for $3,000,000. Three thousand gallons of waterproof coating were rubbed into the limestone surface.

1962 cleaning: (left) applying aluminum paint to the fluting of the tower, (upper right) clean-up worker swinging into platform

Starting with the opening of the New York World's Fair in 1964, the top thirty floors of the Empire State have been bathed in light at night. To begin with, the lights were white. Then, in honor of the Bicentennial, color gels were installed to make the top of the building red, white and blue. When more efficient metal halide lamps went up in 1977 they were designed for color changes. Douglas Leigh, the Times Square billboard wizard, never got a chance to turn the Empire State into a burning cigarette, but he did engineer the lighting. The new lights were inaugurated in blue and white to honor the Yankee's World Series match, and later shifted to red and green for Christmas, red and white for St. Valentine's Day, red, white and blue for Washington's Birthday and July 4, green for St. Patrick's Day, red, white and green for Columbus Day and so forth. Between holidays, the building returns to pure white. When new colors are introduced, men

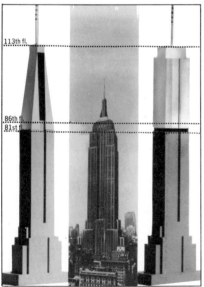

"It's like Chartres!" Robert Jones' models for an extension to the Empire State Building

with walkie-talkies take up positions around the city north, south, east and west of the building, and help electricians on the tower mix the exact shade. New Yorkers are divided about the lighting. Some love it, but others complain that the Empire State has been turned into the world's largest Christmas tree.

In the early 1970's the skyscraper race that had been dead for forty years suddenly sprang to life again. In 1970, the north tower of the World Trade center reached its full height (1,350 feet) and ended the thirty-nine-year reign of the Empire State. The Sears Tower in Chicago (1,450) was soon nearing completion, and Raskob's dreamhouse was about to drop into third place. Robert Jones, of Shreve, Lamb and Harmon, decided to fight back. He called a few engineers, spoke to the owners, and began developing designs to add eleven floors to the Empire State Building. His drawings called for razing the present building above the 81st floor and then adding a new thirty-three story structure. That would bring the total to one-hundred-thirteen stories and 1,494 feet—back in first place. The addition would be in the modern glass and steel style and would contain 300,000–400,000 square feet of free-flowing office space. Mr. Jones had this to say about style:

I think it would be pretentious as hell to do it in the style of the [original] building. If you're going to do something like this, you'd better not get cutesy about it. It's like Chartres. They built one tower in early Gothic and later they built another one in flamboyant Gothic.

One or two questions remained unanswered, though—how to demolish sixteen floors one thousand feet

The 1961 sale: (right) Henry Crown turning over a certain building to Lawrence Wien and Prudential president Louis Menagh

above the street, how to run elevators to the new summit and how to expand the plumbing. Although the plan made the first page of *The Times*, it was never developed in detail, and since the mid-seventies has quietly vanished. The building's fame rests on more than just the current height record.

Along with the exterior changes in the Empire State, there were a few internal ones too. Central air conditioning was installed and the fifty-eight elevators were automated. The building also changed hands—three times. In 1951, a year after Raskob's death, Roger L.

Stevens headed up a group that bought Empire State for $34 million. At the same time, the Prudential Insurance Company bought the land for $17 million. Then in 1954 a Chicago syndicate headed by Colonel Henry Crown bought the building for $51.5 million. In 1961, Prudential, which already held the land, together with a group headed by Lawrence Wien and Harry Helmsley, bought the building for $65 million. This last deal was the most complex in real estate history. Just the agenda for the closing ran to twenty-nine pages, and the formal signing alone took four hours.

SEVEN MILES OF ELEVATOR SHAFTS

LOCATION: West side of Fifth Avenue, between 34th and 33rd Street

DIMENSIONS OF PLOT: 197.5 feet on Fifth Avenue, 424.95 on 34th Street and 33rd Street. (This comprises the plot of the old Waldorf-Astoria and additional land.)

AREA OF SITE: 83,860 square feet.

HEIGHT OF BUILDING: 102 stories above the street, 2 stories below grade. 1,250 feet to the tip of the mooring mast. 1,265 feet to

"vanishing point." Observatory roof at 86th floor. Mooring mast extends 200 feet higher. The building is the tallest structure of any kind in the world. The Eiffel Tower is 984 feet, the Chrysler Building, 1,046 feet to the tip of its spire (habitable only to 783 feet; Empire State is habitable to the very top). The Bank of Manhattan Building is 838 feet, the Woolworth Building 792 feet.

SET BACKS: Only 5 stories of Empire State cover the entire lot area. The tower sets back 60 feet from the lot line above the fifth floor.

CUBIC CONTENTS: 37,000,000 cubic feet.

RENTABLE AREA: 2,158,000 square feet. All space is outside. The building will house 25,000 tenants. Floating population (visitors) is estimated at 40,000 daily. In an emergency 80,000 people could be sheltered.

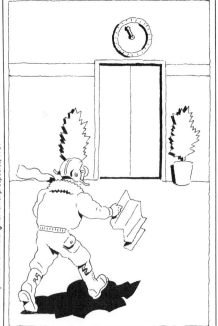

ELEVATORS: 63 passenger elevators and four freight elevators. All are Otis, signal control, self-leveling. Express cars reach the 80th floor in less than one minute. Tower elevators from the 80th floor to the 86th floor, the mast elevator from 86th floor to observatory atop the mooring mast. Elevators rise at a speed of 1,200 feet per minute.

STEEL FRAME: Empire State steel work weighs 60,000 tons, the largest single steel order ever placed for building construction. Loads on individual columns are in excess of 10,000,000 lbs., more than 5,000 tons. Steel work was begun March 17, 1930, and completed in 6 months– a record.

EXTERIOR MASONRY: Indiana limestone and granite with strips of chrome-nickel steel extending from the 6th to the 86th floor. Mooring mast is covered with glass, chrome-nickel steel and aluminum, illuminated from within and carrying a beacon at the top.

An average of 2,500 men were employed daily in Empire State construction work, the maximum number for any one day being about 4,000.

Enough steel has gone into Empire State to build a double track railroad from New York to Saratoga Springs. Four and one-half stories of steel were erected every week. Each steel member reached the building accurately marked to indicate its position and was riveted into place only 80 hours after being fabricated in the mills at Pittsburgh.

More than 17,000,000 feet of telephone and telegraph wire and cable are in Empire State.

Miles of temporary water piping were installed for the convenience of workmen. There are over 50 miles of permanent piping. Four cafeterias supplied food for the army on the job.

Empire State has 6,500 windows, 10,000,000 bricks were used, there are 200,000 cubic feet of stone, 730 tons of exterior chrome-nickel steel and aluminum, nearly 7 miles of elevator shafts, enough floor space to shelter a city of 80,000.

EMPIRE STATEMENTS

Ceci n'est pas l'Empire State Bldg.

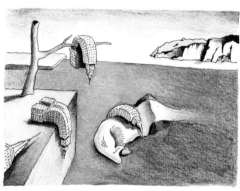

Credits

Edward Sorel

Vito Genovese, Mafia Don